Teaching Notes

Contents

Introduction

Fireflies is an exciting non-fiction series within *Oxford Reading Tree*. These books are specially designed to be used alongside the Stage 6 stories. They provide practice of reading skills in a non-fiction context whilst using the same simple, repetitive sentence structures as the *Oxford Reading Tree* stories. They also contain a selection of decodable and tricky words. Each stage builds on the reading skills and vocabulary from previous stages. Each book offers scope for developing children's word recognition and language comprehension skills in a highly motivating way, whilst also providing strong cross-curricular links.

To help children approach each new book in this stage with confidence, you should prepare the children for reading by talking about the book and asking questions. You can use these Teaching Notes and the additional notes in the inside front and back covers of the pupil books to help you. The notes within the pupil books can also be used by parents or teaching assistants.

Using the books

This booklet provides suggestions for using the books for guided, group and independent activities. The reading activities include ideas for developing children's *word recognition* Ⓦ and *language comprehension* Ⓒ skills. Within word recognition, there are ideas for helping children practise their phonic skills and knowledge, as well as helping them tackle words which are not easy to decode phonically. The language comprehension ideas include suggestions for teaching the skills of prediction, questioning, clarifying, summarising and imagining, in order to help children understand the texts. Suggestions are also provided for speaking and listening and writing activities, as well as for introducing linked electronic material and cross-curricular links.

Reading Fluency

To support children in developing fluency in their reading, you can give them plenty of opportunities to revisit the books. These include:

- rereading independently
- rereading with a partner
- rereading at home
- hearing the book read to them as they follow the printed text.

Rereading and rehearing helps children develop automatic word recognition and gives them models of fluent, expressive reading.

Comprehension strategies

Title	Comprehension strategy taught through these Teaching Notes				
	Prediction	Questioning	Clarifying	Summarising	Imagining
Skateboarding	✓	✓	✓		✓
Wild Weather	✓	✓	✓		✓
Food As Art	✓	✓	✓	✓	✓
Unusual Buildings	✓	✓	✓		✓
Tour de France	✓	✓	✓		✓
Dinosaurs	✓	✓	✓	✓	✓

Vocabulary and phonic opportunities

The chart shows the main words used in each book. The decodable words listed should be decodable for most children at this Stage. The tricky words are common but do not conform to the phonic rules taught up to this point – children will need support to learn and recognise them. If children struggle with one of these words you can model how to read it.

Skateboarding	High frequency decodable words	street, race, trick, ramp, jump(s), scooters, ground, middle, off, on, wheels, air, rollerskates
	High frequency tricky words	skateboarding, skateboard(s), board
Wild Weather	High frequency decodable words	wild, cloud(s), thunder, air, flash, strong, weather, flood, rain, hail, storm, thunderstorm, tornado, hurricane, lightning
	High frequency tricky words	dangerous
Food As Art	High frequency decodable words	picture, sculpture, furniture, artist, stuck, made, painted, food, cakes, this, shows, from, very, different, photograph, walls
	High frequency tricky words	people
Unusual Buildings	High frequency decodable words	houses, made, glass, ago, long, time, bricks, would, bottles, space, unusual, pyramids
	High frequency tricky words	people, warm, built, build, buildings, builders
Tour de France	High frequency decodable words	bike, rider, team(s), mountains, fastest, cyclist, flat, rider, fast, day, hills, France, each, race
	High frequency tricky words	tyre(s), through, jersey, stage(s)
Dinosaurs	High frequency decodable words	big, brain(s), carnivores, herbivores, eggs, beak, feet, teeth, fossils, bird, ate, years, taller
	High frequency tricky words	dinosaurs, Earth

Curriculum coverage chart

	Speaking and listening activities	Reading	Writing
Skateboarding			
PNS Literacy Framework (Y2)	1.3, 3.1	**W** 5.2, 6.1 **C** 7.1, 7.5, 8.2	9.3, 11.1
National Curriculum	Working within Level 2		
Scotland (5–14) (P3)	Level A		
N. Ireland (P3/Y3)	1, 2, 5, 8, 9, 10	1, 3, 6, 8, 16, 17	2, 4, 6, 8, 12
Wales (Key Stage 1)	Range: 1, 2, 3 Skills: 1, 2, 3, 4, 5	Range: 3, 4 Skills: 1, 2, 4	Range: 1, 2, 5, 7 Skills: 1, 4, 5, 6
	Speaking and listening activities	**Reading**	**Writing**
Wild Weather			
PNS Literacy Framework (Y2)	1.1, 1.3, 3.1, 3.2	**W** 5.2, 5.3, 6.1 **C** 7.1, 7.4	9.1, 9.4, 10.1
National Curriculum	Working within Level 2		
Scotland (5–14) (P3)	Level A		
N. Ireland (P3/Y3)	1, 2, 5, 6, 9, 10, 11, 14	1, 3, 6, 8, 15, 16, 17	2, 3, 5, 8, 9
Wales (Key Stage 1)	Range: 1, 2, 3 Skills: 1, 2, 3, 4, 5, 6	Range: 3, 4 Skills: 1, 2, 4	Range: 1, 2, 7 Skills: 1, 2, 4, 5, 6

Key

C = Language comprehension   Y = Year

W = Word recognition   P = Primary

In the designations such as 5.2, the first number represents the strand and the second number the bullet point.

Curriculum coverage chart

	Speaking and listening activities	Reading	Writing
Food As Art			
PNS Literacy Framework (Y2)	1.3, 3.1	**W** 5.2, 5.5, 6.1 **C** 7.3, 7.4, 7.5, 8.3	9.3, 9.5
National Curriculum	Working within Level 2		
Scotland (5–14) (P3)	Level A		
N. Ireland (P3/Y3)	1, 2, 5, 6, 8, 10	1, 3, 6, 8, 15, 16, 17	4, 6, 8, 9, 12
Wales (Key Stage 1)	Range: 1, 2, 3 Skills: 1, 2, 3, 4, 5, 6	Range: 3, 4 Skills: 1, 2, 4	Range: 1, 2, 4, 5, 7 Skills: 1, 5, 6
	Speaking and listening activities	**Reading**	**Writing**
Unusual Buildings			
PNS Literacy Framework (Y2)	2.1, 3.2, 3.3	**W** 5.2, 5.3, 6.1 **C** 7.1, 7.4, 8.3	9.1, 11.1, 11.2
National Curriculum	Working within Level 2		
Scotland (5–14) (P3)	Level A		
N. Ireland (P3/Y3)	1, 2, 5, 6, 8, 10, 12	1, 3, 8, 11, 12, 15, 16, 17	3, 4, 5, 6, 9, 12
Wales (Key Stage 1)	Range: 1, 2, 3 Skills: 1, 2, 3, 4, 5, 6	Range: 3, 4 Skills: 1, 2, 4	Range: 1, 2, 5, 7 Skills: 1, 5, 6

Curriculum coverage chart

	Speaking and listening activities	Reading	Writing
Tour de France			
PNS Literacy Framework (Y2)	1.1, 3.1, 3.2	**W** 5.3, 5.4, 5.5 **C** 7.1, 7.3, 8.3	9.2, 9.3, 12.3
National Curriculum	Working within Level 2		
Scotland (5–14) (P3)	Level A		
N. Ireland (P3/Y3)	1, 2, 5, 6, 8, 10, 12	1, 3, 8, 14, 15, 16, 17	1, 2, 5, 7, 8
Wales (Key Stage 1)	Range: 1, 2, 3 Skills: 1, 2, 3, 4, 5, 6	Range: 3, 4 Skills: 1, 2, 4	Range: 1, 2, 3, 7 Skills: 1, 4, 5
	Speaking and listening activities	**Reading**	**Writing**
Dinosaurs			
PNS Literacy Framework (Y2)	1.3, 3.1	**W** 5.1, 5.2, 6.1 **C** 7.1, 7.3, 7.4, 8.3	9.3, 11.1, 12.1
National Curriculum	Working within Level 2		
Scotland (5–14) (P3)	Level A		
N. Ireland (P3/Y3)	1, 2, 5, 6, 8, 10	1, 3, 8, 14, 15, 16, 17	4, 5, 6, 7, 12, 13
Wales (Key Stage 1)	Range: 1, 2, 3 Skills: 1, 2, 3, 4, 5, 6	Range: 3, 4 Skills: 1, 2, 4	Range: 1, 2, 7 Skills: 1, 2, 5, 6, 7

Skateboarding

> **C** = Language comprehension   **R, AF** = QCA Reading assessment focus
>
> **W** = Word recognition   **W, AF** = QCA Writing assessment focus

Group or guided reading

Introducing the book

C *(Clarifying)* Encourage the children to explore the cover. They should look for clues, like detectives. Is the book fiction or non-fiction? Prompt them to consider the photograph and how this suggests non-fiction.

C *(Prediction)* Ask the children to say what information they think they will find in this book.

W Ask the children to identify the two smaller words in the title ('skate' and 'board'). Talk about why the sport has this name.

C *(Clarifying)* Look through the book. Prompt the children to see that every page tells us something new about skateboarding.

Strategy check

Remind the children to use their knowledge of phonics to work out new words.

Independent reading

C *(Questioning)* Ask the children to look for the Contents page. Explain that it shows us what is in the book and where to find it. Ask: *On which page can we find information on the history of skateboarding? Where do we find information on skateboarding tricks?*

W Look at 'Xtreme Skateboarding' in the Contents. Discuss why 'extreme' might be spelt in this way (consider 'X-ray', 'Xmas').

C *(Clarifying)* Ask the children to find the Introduction. Explain that it is near the beginning of the book and tells us that there are two types of skateboarding. Explore the differences between 'street' and 'ramp' skateboarding.

C *(Clarifying)* On pages 4 and 5, talk about the diagram. Explain that a 'diagram' shows a plan or an outline of something. If possible, illustrate by comparing the diagram with the view of the skateboard on page 17. Identify its different parts, e.g. 'trucks', 'tail'.

W Encourage the children to read independently, using their phonic knowledge to tackle unfamiliar words. Help them with unfamiliar terms, e.g. 'wheelie', 'stalefish', etc.

Assessment Check that children:

- *(R, AF1)* use a variety of strategies to work out new words
- *(R, AF1)* read high and medium frequency words automatically
- *(R, AF4)* take account of commas.

Returning to the text

C *(Questioning)* Ask the children: *How do people do street skateboarding? What special things do they need for ramp skateboarding? How many different jumps are described?*

W Look at the time line on pages 10–11. Ask: *Can you find a word that means 'started'?*

W Encourage the children to identify the letters that make the 'ai' sound in 'skateboard' (a-e). Ask them to find words in which the 'ai' sound is spelt differently on pages 15 and 17 ('rail' and 'taildrag').

C *(Imagining)* Ask the children to say which skateboarding trick they think could be the most dangerous, and why.

Group and independent reading activities

Objective Draw together ideas and information from across a whole text, using simple signposts in the text (7.1).

C *(Questioning)* Ask the children 'when' questions, such as:

When did people first get interested in skateboarding? When did it become a popular sport? When did people start to call skateboarding an 'Xtreme sport'?

Assessment *(R, AF2)* Do the children use the Contents to find the 'History' and 'Time Line' pages?

| Objective | Explore how particular words are used, including words and expressions with similar meanings (7.5). |

W Explore familiar words that have a new meaning in relation to skateboarding: 'neck', 'nose', 'tail', etc.

With the children's help, make a topic list of skateboarding 'jump' words and read them together.

| Assessment | *(R, AF2)* Do the children retrieve relevant words? |

| Objective | Engage with books through exploring interpretations (8.2). |

C *(Clarifying)* Ask the children: *If a skateboarder tries an 'ollie', what do they need to do first? How does a 'wheelie' turn into a 'taildrag'?*

Encourage the children to work in pairs to explain a trick to each other without naming it. The listener must guess which trick is being described.

| Assessment | *(R, AF2)* Are the children able to describe the tricks clearly? |

| Objective | Spell with increasing accuracy and confidence, drawing on word recognition and knowledge of word structure and spelling patterns (5.2, 6.1). |

W Ask the children to find the most important '-ing' word in the book. How often is 'skateboarding' used? How many other words ending in '-ing' can they find?

Encourage the children to work in small groups – while one person reads each '-ing' word from the book, the others write it down.

| Assessment | *(W, AF8)* Do the children use correct spellings? |

eFireflies

This book is available electronically, on *eFireflies* Stages 6–10 CD-ROM. You can read the text as a 'Talking Book' on a whiteboard with the whole class, or on a computer with a group of children. Use the tools to annotate the text with the children. The children can then use 'Make a Book' to select their own choice of content and make their own books. Use the Teacher Settings screen to select how you want any part of the CD-ROM to be used, and the Progress Report Chart to track the progress of individual children.

Speaking and listening activities

Objective Explain ideas and processes using imaginative and adventurous vocabulary (1.3).

Ensure that everyone contributes (3.1).

You will need a skateboard and safety gear.

- One group explains the various parts of a skateboard, using the correct terms. Another group presents the safety items. Get them to show how they are used and explain why they are needed.

- Ask the children to describe their favourite jump. Ask: *How do you do it? How would you feel if you were doing an 'ollie'?* Encourage expressive words, e.g. 'excited', 'scared', 'proud', and the use of non-verbal gestures to describe the jump.

Cross-curricular links: National Curriculum Key Stage 1

Design and Technology

Pupils should be taught to:

- Communicate their ideas using a variety of methods, including drawing and making models.

Writing activities

Objective Maintain consistency in narrative, including purpose and tense (9.3). Write simple and compound sentences (11.1).

Using the book as a model, ask the children to write out instructions for performing a complicated jump, e.g. the powerslide.

Encourage them to include an introductory paragraph about the sport, and a diagram with arrows and labels identifying parts of a board.

Assessment *(W, AF3)* Do the children sequence the information correctly and structure the page effectively?

Wild Weather

C = Language comprehension	**R, AF** = QCA Reading assessment focus	
W = Word recognition	**W, AF** = QCA Writing assessment focus	

Group or guided reading

Introducing the book

C *(Questioning)* Introduce the book by asking the children to describe today's weather. Ask: *Is it wild, fine or in-between?*

W Read the title, 'Wild Weather' and discuss the kinds of weather this book might tell us about. Think of another word that means 'wild' in connection with the weather, e.g. 'fierce', 'angry', 'violent'.

C *(Clarifying)* Tell the children that 'Wild Weather' is an information book. Ask: *Does this mean fiction or non-fiction?*

C *(Clarifying)* Look briefly at the Glossary and Index on pages 23 and 24. Explain how each is used if necessary. Point to the word 'hail' in bold on page 4 and explain that this means that the meaning of the word can be found in the Glossary.

Strategy check

Remind the children to use their knowledge of sounds and spelling patterns to work out unfamiliar words.

Independent reading

C *(Prediction)* Read the Contents list. Ask the children to guess which storm is the biggest and strongest. Suggest that they look through the book to find out.

C *(Clarifying)* Look at page 3. Ask: *Do you think this paragraph reads like an introduction? Can you say why?* (It gives the reader an idea of what the rest of the book is about.)

W There are lots of sound words in this book. The first, on page 3, 'Woosh!' tells us how a big storm might sound. Ask the children to look out for more sound words as they read the book.

(C) *(Clarifying)* On page 3, introduce the exclamation mark. Explain that it tells us to read certain words with expression, e.g. in a loud voice or sounding surprised. Ask: *Can you think of other words that often use an exclamation mark to make them seem important?* (e.g. Danger! Fire! Help!)

(W) Check that they can read the phonemes 'au' as in 'caused' and 'ew' as in 'blew'. Help them to break down compound words, e.g. 'thunderstorm', 'motorway'.

Assessment Check that children:

- *(R, AF1)* use a variety of strategies to work out new words
- *(R, AF1)* read high and medium frequency words automatically
- *(R, AF4)* use expression appropriate to exclamation marks.

Returning to the text

(C) *(Questioning)* Ask the children: *What kind of storm uses a sight word? Which storm has an 'eye'? Which kind of wild storms are called 'twisters'?*

(W) Look at the word 'lightning' and ask the children to identify the sound made by the trigraph 'igh'. Ask the children to find the same trigraph on page 10 ('high') and a different trigraph on page 14 ('tch' in 'stretch').

(C) *(Clarifying)* Encourage the children to look up 'clouds' and 'twister' using the Index. Ask: *What does the book tell you about clouds and twisters?*

(C) *(Imagining)* Ask the children to say which type of weather might be the most frightening, and why.

Group and independent reading activities

Objective Draw together ideas and information from across a whole text, using simple signposts in the text (7.1).

(C) *(Questioning)* Ask the children to answer the following questions using the direct style of the text.

Why do you see lightning before you hear thunder rumbling? What can winds make in the ocean? What is a tornado?

Assessment *(R, AF2)* Do the children use the Index and Glossary to find their answers?

Objective Speak with clarity and use appropriate intonation (1.1).

Ⓦ Look at the way exclamation marks are used on page 8. Encourage children to read the page aloud, with appropriate expression.

Assessment *(R, AF1)* Do the children read the high frequency words without hesitation and use the correct emphasis? *(R, AF4)* Do the children correctly emphasise the words in capitals but not the glossary words in bold?

Objective Spell with increasing accuracy and confidence, drawing on word recognition and knowledge of word structure and spelling patterns (5.2, 6.1).

Ⓦ Ask the children to find words within words. Can they spot common endings (e.g. '-ing', '-ed' and 's')?

Return to page 8 and ask the children how to turn 'rumble' and 'crackle' into '-ing' words. Encourage them to spell them out for you to write on the board. Then change them into words ending in '-ed'.

Assessment *(W, AF8)* Do the children use correct spellings?

Objective Know how to tackle unfamiliar words that are not completely decodable (5.3).
Use syntax and context to build their store of vocabulary when reading for meaning (7.4).

Ⓦ Look at the glossary and explore unfamiliar words. Write out a list of new words for wild weather.

Assessment *(AF1)* Do the children use their phonic knowledge to tackle words that are not completely decodable?

Speaking and listening activities

Objective Explain ideas and processes using imaginative and adventurous vocabulary (1.3).
Ensure that everyone contributes (3.1).
Work effectively in groups (3.2).

You will need enlarged photographs from the book.

- Using photographs, ask one group to choose two weather types, e.g. a hurricane and a tornado, and to explain the difference.
- Give them time to prepare what they will say and to decide which group members will present different information. Encourage them to use interesting vocabulary, e.g. sound words, to describe each weather type.
- Invite another group to listen and comment.

Cross-curricular links: National Curriculum Key Stage 1

Geography

Pupils should be taught to:

- Use geographical vocabulary.

Writing activities

Objective Draw on knowledge and experience of texts in deciding and planning how and what to write (9.1).
Use planning to establish clear sections for writing (10.1).

Encourage the children to plan and write a wild weather book of their own, in zigzag form, explaining how different storms are caused. Encourage them to use features from *Wild Weather*, such as pictures, captions, Glossary and Index.

Assessment *(W, AF3)* Do the children structure their book and use presentational features effectively?

Objective Make adventurous word and language choices appropriate to the style and purpose of the text (9.4).

Encourage the children to make up a chant using sound words for weather, e.g.
Woosh! goes the wind,
Splash! comes the rain,
Crash! goes the thunder,
Boom! it comes again!

Assessment *(W, AF7)* Do the children select effective vocabulary?

Food As Art

C = Language comprehension	*R, AF* = QCA Reading assessment focus
W = Word recognition	*W, AF* = QCA Writing assessment focus

Group or guided reading

Introducing the book

C *(Prediction)* Before showing the children the book, tell them the title and ask them to guess what the book is about. Settle for something like 'making pictures with food'.

C *(Questioning, Imagining)* Now encourage the children to explore the cover and look for more clues. Ask: *Can you identify the food in this picture? How do you think it might taste?*

W Ask the children to read the blurb on the back of the book. Ask them to find two words with the same 'oo' sound but spelt differently ('food' and 'you').

W Ask the children to find the author's name on the front of the book and encourage them to have a go at reading it, using their knowledge of letter sounds to help them.

Strategy check

Remind the children to use their knowledge of phonics to work out new words.

Independent reading

W Encourage the children to read independently, using their phonic knowledge to tackle unfamiliar words.

C *(Clarifying)* Read the Contents. How many different foods are listed? Discuss what is meant by 'Food Art at Home'.

C *(Summarising, Clarifying)* After reading the Introduction on page 3, ask the children to name the three different kinds of artists that are mentioned. Discuss with the children how sculptors, painters and photographers work.

(C) *(Questioning, Clarifying)* Before you read on, ask the children to think of some food art they could make at home (e.g. birthday cakes, pasta mosaics).

(C) *(Prediction)* Look at the photographs on pages 4–5. Ask: *What kind of food has been used to make these pictures?*

(C) *(Questioning)* Encourage the children to describe how the layout of the text on pages 17–23 is different, e.g. lists, numbered pictures and texts.

Assessment Check that children:

- *(R, AF1)* use a variety of strategies to make sense of their reading
- *(R, AF1)* read high and medium frequency words automatically
- *(R, AF4)* are able to comment on the organisation and layout of the text.

Returning to the text

(C) *(Questioning)* Ask the children: *Why can't you eat the profiterole on page 11? What happens to butter on a hot day? What ingredients do you need to make play dough?*

(W) Ask: *How many verbs using the past tense ending '-ed' can you find throughout the book?*

(W) On page 5, ask the children to identify the letters that make the 'oo' sound in 'room'. Ask them to find the same sound in another word in the first sentence ('blue'). On page 7, ask them to find the same word with the same sound but spelt differently ('chew').

(C) *(Clarifying)* On page 23, encourage the children to find recipe words that tell you what to do, e.g. 'stir', 'mix', 'roll'. Ask: *Can you think of any more words like this?* (e.g. 'whisk', 'blend')

Group and independent reading activities

Objective Explain organisational features of texts, including alphabetical order, layout, captions (7.3).

(C) *(Questioning)* Encourage the children to describe and explain the organisational features of the book. Ask: *How are arrows used throughout the book? Which text is numbered? Why are some* *photographs numbered? Can you find any lists? Why are lists used? Which text is in alphabetical order?*

Assessment *(R, AF4)* Do the children identify the features, and notice that the instructional text uses special features such as numbers?

Objective Use syntax and context to build their store of vocabulary when reading for meaning (7.4).

C Can the children find a linking word on page 8? ('When' links one sentence to the next.) Can the children find a linking word on page 5? ('But' links one sentence to the next.)

Assessment *(R, AF1)* Do the children identify the linking words?

Objective Read high and medium frequency words independently and automatically (5.5).

W Look at the word 'photograph' on page 4. Help the children to identify the 'ph' sound. Let them leaf through the text to find and sight-read the word each time it appears.

Assessment *(R, AF1)* Are the children able to find and read the word quickly?

Objective Spell with increasing accuracy and confidence, drawing on word recognition and knowledge of word structure and spelling patterns (5.2, 6.1).

W Help the children to practise new words related to food. Encourage them to find suitable words in the book and help you to spell the words correctly as you write them on the board.

Assessment *(W, AF8)* Do the children use correct spellings?

Objective Read high and medium frequency words independently and automatically (5.5).

Explore how particular words are used, including words and expressions with similar meanings (7.5).

W Look at the Introduction. The author says, 'Some artists use food...'. Later she says: 'used', 'painted' and 'covered'. Tell the children that these words are in the past tense. Explore the reasons for this. Can they find more past-tense words ending in '-ed'?

Assessment *(R, AF1)* Do the children find the '-ed' endings quickly?

Speaking and listening activities

Objective Explain ideas and processes using imaginative and adventurous vocabulary (1.3).
Ensure that everyone contributes (3.1).
Explain their reactions to texts, commenting on important aspects (8.3).

- Invite children to explain how different foods could be used to make art. Encourage others to comment and invent alternative ideas.

- Hold a class discussion about the book. Ask: *Do you think the author has told us enough about art made from food? What more would you like to have read about?*

Cross-curricular links: National Curriculum Key Stage 1

Art and Design

Pupils should be taught about:

- Materials and processes used in making art, craft and design.

Writing activities

Objective Maintain consistency in narrative, including purpose and tense (9.3).
Select from different presentational features to suit particular writing purposes on screen and on paper (9.5).

Following the pattern of instructions for making pasta jewellery or play dough, encourage the children to plan and write out their own set of instructions for making potato prints. Remind them to use the appropriate presentational features for an instruction text.

Assessment *(W, AF3)* Do the children sequence the information correctly and include a list of what you need?

Unusual Buildings

> **C** = Language comprehension   *R, AF* = QCA Reading assessment focus
>
> **W** = Word recognition   *W, AF* = QCA Writing assessment focus

Group or guided reading

Introducing the book

C *(Questioning)* Look at the cover and discuss the title. Ask: *What is unusual or strange about the building on the cover?*

C *(Prediction)* Before looking inside the book, ask the children to suggest more unusual buildings that might be described in the book (e.g. The Dome, Big Ben, The Eiffel Tower).

Strategy check

Remind the children to use their knowledge of phonics to work out unfamiliar words.

Independent reading

● Encourage the children to read the text using their knowledge of phonics to tackle unfamiliar words, and to break up compound words into their parts (e.g. 'futuristic', 'materials', 'igloos').

C *(Questioning)* Go to pages 4–5. Talk about why pyramids look unusual to us. Ask: *Which part of a modern house usually has a triangular shape?*

C *(Clarifying, Questioning)* Encourage the children to find another page that shows a building from history (Leaning Tower of Pisa, page 14). Ask: *Why is it unusual? Why does it lean?*

C *(Clarifying)* Ask the children to find pages that show houses built from very unusual materials. On pages 10–11, ask: *How do the bottles keep the house warm at night?* On page 12, ask: *What other objects might the castle be made of?* (e.g. tins, old cars)

C *(Clarifying)* Discuss what is very unusual about the building on pages 16–17.

C Ask the children to find a page that shows a building of the future.

Assessment Check that children:

- *(R, AF1)* use a variety of strategies to work out new words
- *(R, AF1)* read high and medium frequency words automatically
- *(R, AF4)* use the correct intonation for the questions on page 22.

Returning to the text

C *(Imagining)* Ask the children: *Which of the unusual buildings would you like to live in? What makes your choice a particularly strange building? What might a house built on the moon look like?*

W Talk about the word 'unusual' and ask the children to suggest alternatives, e.g. 'weird', 'different', 'fantastic'.

W Point out how the word 'unusual' can be split into parts. Explain that the prefix 'un-' means 'not'. Ask: *Can you think of more words beginning with 'un-' meaning 'not'?* (e.g. 'unhappy', 'unstuck', 'unnecessary')

C *(Clarifying)* Open the book and read the Introduction. Explain that an introduction is a statement of purpose, i.e. it tells you what the book sets out to do. Ask: *Does this introduction work?*

Group and independent reading activities

Objective Draw together ideas and information from across a whole text, using simple signposts in the text (7.1).
Explain their reactions to texts, commenting on important aspects (8.3).

C *(Questioning)* Ask the children: *Why might a building that looks strange to you not look strange to someone else?*

Assessment *(R, AF2)* Do the children refer to details in the text to help answer the questions?

Objective Draw on knowledge and experience of texts in deciding and planning what and how to write (9.1).

W Ask the children to read the text on page 4. It tells us about the pyramids and why they were built. Ask: *Can you think of a good question to add to the text on this page?*

Turn to pages 6–7 and cover up the caption. Read the text on page 7 and ask the children to suggest a caption for the photograph.

Ask them to write down their caption. Compare their caption with the one on page 6.

Assessment *(R, AF3)* Do the children suggest an appropriate question and caption for this non-fiction text?

Objective Know how to tackle unfamiliar words that are not completely decodable (5.3).

Ⓦ Look at some unfamiliar words in the text (e.g. 'adobe') and ask the children to find out what they mean. Encourage them to suggest how to pronounce any words that are new to them.

Assessment *(R, AF1)* Do the children use their phonic knowledge to work out new words?

Objective Spell with increasing accuracy and confidence, drawing on word recognition and knowledge of word structure and spelling patterns (5.2, 6.1).

Ⓦ Ask the children to write a list of junk building materials. Encourage them to add their own ideas. Remind them to use their knowledge of letter sounds to spell the words correctly.

Assessment *(W, AF8)* Do the children use correct spellings?

Objective Know how to tackle unfamiliar words that are not completely decodable (5.3).
Use syntax and context to build their store of vocabulary when reading for meaning (7.4).

Ⓦ Make a list of unfamiliar words from the book. Put them in alphabetical order and add meanings to make a Glossary.

Assessment *(R, AF1)* Do the children use their phonic knowledge to tackle words that are not completely decodable?

E-links

Fireflies Plus

If you are an Espresso user, you can access cross-curricular videos and multimedia activities (including writing opportunities and quizzes) linked to this title to enrich your children's reading. Children can also write, post and compare reviews of the book. Full supporting

Teaching Notes for this content are available on the site in PDF format. Within the Espresso site, follow the route **<Channel guide → English 1 → Oxford Reading Tree Fireflies Plus logo>**. *Espresso Primary* is an extensive library of cross-curricular video-rich broadband teaching resources and learning activities that motivates children and supports teachers.

Speaking and listening activities

Objective Listen to others in class, ask relevant questions (2.1).
Work effectively in groups (3.2).
Listen to each other's views and preferences (3.3).

You will need enlarged photographs of buildings in the book, and pictures of other interesting buildings, e.g. Sydney Opera House.

● Hold a group discussion on which building is the most unusual. Children can take turns to choose a building and explain why they think it is the most unusual. Encourage other children to ask questions about their choice. Hold a group vote on which building is 'the most unusual'.

Cross-curricular links: National Curriculum Key Stage 1

Art and Design

Pupils should be taught to:

● Talk about their ideas, saying what they like and dislike.

Writing activities

Objective Draw on knowledge and experience of texts in deciding and planning how and what to write (9.1).
Write simple and compound sentences (11.1).
Compose sentences using present tense consistently (11.2).

Ask the children to draw an unusual house. Encourage them to write simple and compound sentences to accompany the drawing, using a direct impersonal style, and to add a caption.

Assessment *(W, AF2)* Do the children use tense consistently?

Tour de France

> **C** = Language comprehension   *R, AF* = QCA Reading assessment focus
>
> **W** = Word recognition   *W, AF* = QCA Writing assessment focus

Group or guided reading

Introducing the book

W Look at the cover and read the title with the children. Suggest they look closely at the word 'de'. Ask: *Have you ever seen it before?* Tell them that it is a French word meaning 'of'. Prompt them to translate the title into English.

C *(Prediction)* Read the Introduction to discover what kind of race the Tour de France is. Ask the children to predict what information about the race they think they will discover (e.g. the bikes, the riders). Read the Contents on page 2 and compare it with their prediction.

W Look together at page 3. Ask: *What is the name for the text at the beginning of the book that tells you what it's about?* Read the word 'Introduction', encouraging the child to tackle it by splitting it into syllables.

Strategy check

Remind the children to use their knowledge of sounds and spelling patterns to work out unfamiliar words.

Independent reading

C *(Questioning)* Look at the Contents, and turn to the page headed 'Prizes'. Ask: *What unusual prizes are awarded in the Tour de France?*

W On page 3, check that the children can identify the long 'i' sound in 'bike'. On page 7, ask them to find the same 'i' sound but with a different spelling ('tyre').

C *(Clarifying)* On page 7, can the children answer the question at the top of the page? Ask: *What do you need to mend a flat tyre?*

C *(Clarifying)* Read the pages describing the course and track it on the map. Ask: *Is the information the same on page 8 as on page 9?* Think about how each is presented.

C *(Questioning)* Look at page 12. Ask: *What does the text tell us about the special bikes that the Tour de France athletes use?*

Assessment Check that children:

- *(R, AF1)* use a variety of strategies to work out new words
- *(R, AF1)* read high and medium frequency words automatically
- *(R, AF4)* can describe the different layout and presentational features (map, labels, etc.).

Returning to the text

C *(Questioning)* Ask the children:
How many stages are there in the race?
Where does the Tour de France finish?
What colour jersey does the winner get to keep?

W Read the text on page 13. Point to 'Wheel' and ask the children to point to the long 'ee' sound. Ask them to find the same sound in another word on the page ('lever').

C *(Imagining)* Turn to pages 22–23. Talk about Lance Armstrong. Ask them how Lance Armstrong might have felt after he recovered from a serious illness and went on to win.

Group and independent reading activities

Objective Draw together ideas and information from across a whole text, using simple signposts in the text (7.1).

C *(Questioning)* Ask the children: *What sort of jersey does the race leader wear? What is the rider who wears a red and white polka dot jersey called?*

Assessment *(R, AF2)* Do the children use the Index to find their answers?

Objective Speak with clarity and use appropriate intonation (1.1). Know how to tackle unfamiliar words that are not completely decodable (5.3). Explain organisational features of texts (7.3).

C *(Clarifying)* On page 8, the route is shown by a green line. Ask: *Can you follow the route? Why is there an aircraft logo on the map?*

W Ask volunteers to describe the route by referring to the map. Encourage children to help with the pronunciation of some of the place names.

Assessment *(R, AF1)* Do the children use their phonic knowledge to tackle difficult words?

Objective Read and spell less common alternative graphemes (5.4).

W Ask the children to look through the book to find words to complete two lists: one list of words containing the 'ee' sound and one containing the long 'i' sound.

● Challenge the children to find and list words containing trigraphs, e.g. 'Tour', 'wear'.

Assessment *(W, AF8)* Do the children identify sounds correctly?

Objective Read high and medium frequency words independently and automatically (5.5).

W Point to high and medium frequency words and encourage the children to read them on sight (e.g. 'take', 'goes', 'with', 'race', 'tyres', 'bike' and 'prizes').

Assessment *(AF1)* Can the children read the words without hesitation?

Speaking and listening activities

Objective Ensure that everyone contributes (3.1).
Work effectively in groups (3.2).
Explain their reactions to texts (8.3).

● Talk about the special cycles the competitors use.

● Encourage the children to ask and answer questions about the coloured jerseys.

- Ask the children: *Which part of the book is the most interesting or exciting, and why? Do you think the author has made this race sound really exciting?* Ask groups to discuss and decide what else the book could have included to make it more exciting, e.g. more about the riders, more record-breaker facts, dramatic photos.

Cross-curricular links: National Curriculum Key Stage 1

PE

Pupils should be taught to:

- Recognise and describe how their bodies feel during different activities.

Writing activities

Objective Maintain consistency in non-narrative, including use of person and time (9.3).

- Encourage the children to write a first-person diary account of someone taking part in the race. Encourage them to use imaginative vocabulary.

Assessment *(W, AF2)* Do the children use the first person consistently?

Objective Sustain form in narrative, including use of person and time (9.2). Word-process short narrative and non-narrative texts (12.3).

- Ask the children to write a story about winning a prize on the Tour de France. Encourage them to write about the roar of the crowd and how happy but exhausted they would feel. Ask them to write and edit their work using a word processor.

Assessment *(W, AF7)* Do the children select effective vocabulary?

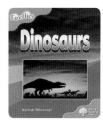

Dinosaurs

C = Language comprehension   *R, AF* = QCA Reading assessment focus

W = Word recognition   *W, AF* = QCA Writing assessment focus

Group or guided reading

Introducing the book

C *(Questioning, Prediction)* Encourage the children to explore the cover, looking for clues. Ask: *What is the book about? Is it fiction or non-fiction?* Discuss why they came to their conclusion.

W Can the children find the name of the author? Encourage them to use their phonic knowledge to read the author's name.

C *(Clarifying)* Leaf through the book, prompting children to identify it as an information book which tells us all about dinosaurs.

Strategy check

Remind the children to use their knowledge of phonics to work out new words.

Independent reading

C *(Clarifying)* Look at the Contents page and explain that it shows what is in the book and where to find it. Ask the children to look up the page about 'Eggs', 'Tracks' and so on, checking that they understand how to use the list.

C *(Questioning)* Read the Introduction on page 3. Ask the children: *What kind of creatures were dinosaurs? Can you think of some reptiles that you could see today?*

W Encourage the children to read independently, helping with the names of the dinosaurs. Remind the children to split them up into syllables, reading one at a time, then blending. Get the children to practise saying them aloud.

C *(Questioning)* Look at the Index on page 24. Ask: *In what way is the Index different from the Contents list?*

(R, AF1) Check that children:

- use a variety of strategies to work out new words
- read on sight high frequency words
- are able to extend their vocabulary by recognising and using unfamiliar words linked to a topic.

Returning to the text

C (Questioning) Ask the children: *Where did the dinosaurs lay their eggs? Which dinosaur is said to be one of the fiercest? Why would Brachiosaurus be one of the safest dinosaurs to meet? How do we know that dinosaurs were ancestors of the birds? What does the Psittacosaurus look like?*

C (Clarifying, Imagining) Discuss the size comparisons on pages 4–5 and ask the children to suggest suitable alternatives.

C (Questioning) Look at pages 6–7 and ask the children to describe carnivores. Turn to pages 9 and 10 and ask: *What were plant-eating dinosaurs called?*

W Ask: *How many verbs using the past-tense ending '-ed' can you find on pages 8–9?*

C (Questioning) Ask: *Which dinosaurs would you least like to meet and why? Does the author tell you enough about what the dinosaurs looked like? Does the book make you want to learn more about them? If it does, where would you look for more information?*

C (Summarising) Ask the children to describe the contents of the book in two or three sentences.

Group and independent reading activities

Objective Read independently and with increasing fluency longer and less familiar texts (5.1).
Draw together ideas and information from across a whole text (7.1).

C (Questioning) Ask the children to reread the relevant pages to find the answers to these questions: *Why do some people think that dinosaurs were able to live on Earth for a very long time? How can we tell that* *birds developed from dinosaurs? Why do scientists think that the dinosaurs died out? How do fossils help us to learn about dinosaurs?*

Assessment *(R, AF2)* Do the children refer to the text when answering these questions? Do they use the Contents to help find the answers?

Objective Explain organisational features of texts (7.3).

C *(Clarifying)* Encourage the children to study the map on page 3. Ask: *What does the map tell us about where dinosaurs once lived?* Ask why this information has been shown as a map. Ask them how else it could have been shown (e.g. list of countries, ordinary text).

Assessment *(R, AF3)* Do the children understand that dinosaurs lived all around the world?

Objective Use syntax and context to build their store of vocabulary (7.4). Draw together ideas and information from across a simple whole text (7.1).

C Look at the Index. Show the children how the dinosaur names are written in alphabetical order. With the children's help, make a topic list of dinosaurs for the wall. Use alphabetical order.

Assessment *(R, AF3)* Do the children suggest appropriate words from the book for topic headings?

Objective Spell with increasing accuracy and confidence, drawing on word recognition and knowledge of word structure and spelling patterns (5.2, 6.1).

W Ask the children to take it in turns to read a dinosaur name for the others to write down and attempt to spell correctly.

Assessment *(R, AF1)* Do the children tackle the words using their phonic knowledge? *(W, AF8)* Do they use correct spelling?

E-links

Fireflies Plus

If you are an Espresso user, you can access cross-curricular videos and multimedia activities (including writing opportunities and quizzes) linked to this title to enrich your children's reading. Children can also write, post and compare reviews of the book. Full supporting

Teaching Notes for this content are available on the site in PDF format. Within the Espresso site, follow the route **<Channel guide → English 1 → Oxford Reading Tree Fireflies Plus logo>**. *Espresso Primary* is an extensive library of cross-curricular, video-rich broadband teaching resources and learning activities that motivates children and supports teachers.

Speaking and listening activities

Objective Explain ideas and processes using imaginative and adventurous vocabulary (1.3).
Ensure that everyone contributes (3.1).

- Divide the class into two groups. One group should describe a very small dinosaur, inviting new size comparisons, e.g. 'as small as a baby lamb'. The other group should contrast this with a description of some extremely large dinosaurs, e.g. 'as big as a double-decker bus'.

Objective Explain their reactions to texts, commenting on important aspects (8.3).

- Encourage the children to take part in a discussion about dinosaurs they would and would not like to see if they were alive today.

Cross-curricular links: National Curriculum Key Stage 1

Sc 2 Science

Pupils should be taught to:

- Group living things according to observable similarities and differences.

Writing activities

Objective Write simple and compound sentences (11.1).
Write legibly, using upper and lower case letters appropriately within words (12.1).

Encourage the children to write and illustrate non-fiction zigzag books describing four different dinosaurs. Encourage them to handwrite their text and to include illustrations and labels.

Assessment *(W, AF3)* Do the children structure the information effectively?

Oxford Reading Tree resources at this level

Biff, Chip and Kipper
Stage 6 Stories
Stage 6 More Stories A
Stage 6 More Stories B
Stage 6 More Stories C

Phonics
Stage 6 Songbirds

Poetry
Glow-worms Stage 5–6

Non-fiction
Stage 6 Fireflies

Wider reading
Stage 6 Snapdragons

Electronic
Stage 6–7 Talking Stories
e-Songbirds
e-Fireflies
MagicPage
Clip Art
ORT Online www.OxfordReadingTree.com

Teachers' Resources
Comprehension Photocopy Masters
(Stages 6–9)
Context Cards
Teacher's Handbook (Stages 1–9)
Group Activity Sheets
Phonics and Spelling Activities (Stages 1–9)
Stage 6 Workbooks

Stage 6–7 Storytapes

Songbirds Teaching Notes, Guided Reading
Cards and Parent Notes

Snapdragons Teaching Notes, Guided
Reading Cards and Parent Notes

Fireflies Teaching Notes

OXFORD
UNIVERSITY PRESS

Great Clarendon Street, Oxford OX2 6DP

Oxford University Press is a department of the University of
Oxford. It furthers the University's objective of excellence in
research, scholarship, and education by publishing worldwide in

Oxford   New York

Auckland   Cape Town   Dar es Salaam   Hong Kong   Karachi
Kuala Lumpur   Madrid   Melbourne   Mexico City   Nairobi
New Delhi   Shanghai   Taipei   Toronto

With offices in

Argentina   Austria   Brazil   Chile   Czech Republic   France
Greece   Guatemala   Hungary   Italy   Japan   Poland
Portugal   Singapore   South Korea   Switzerland
Thailand   Turkey   Ukraine   Vietnam

Oxford is a registered trade mark of Oxford University Press
in the UK and in certain other countries

Text © Oxford University Press 2008

Written by Liz Miles.

The moral rights of the author have been asserted

Database right Oxford University Press (maker)

First published 2008

British Library Cataloguing in Publication Data

Data available

ISBN: 978-0-19-847305-3

10 9 8 7 6 5 4

Page make-up by Thomson Digital

Printed in China by Imago

Paper used in the production of this book is a natural, recyclable
product made from wood grown in sustainable forests. The
manufacturing process conforms to the environmental
regulations of the country of origin.